POOP for BREAKFAST

WHY SOME ANIMALS EAT IT

SARA LEVINE

illustrated by FLORENCE WEISER

M Millbrook Press / Minneapolis

For my dad.

With special thanks to Oliver and Matthew, whose keen observations and questions gave me the idea for this book. —S.L.

For my niece Alice, so curious to know everything, even more when it's funny. —F.W.

Millbrook Press™
An imprint of Lerner Publishing Group, Inc.
241 First Avenue North
Minneapolis, MN 55401 USA

For reading levels and more information, look up this title at www.lernerbooks.com.

Designed by Kimberly Morales.
Main body text set in Billy Infant. Typeface provided by SparkyType.
The illustrations in this book were created with pencils and paper, and Procreate.

Library of Congress Cataloging-in-Publication Data

Names: Levine, Sara (Veterinarian), author. | Weiser, Florence, illustrator.
Title: Poop for breakfast : why some animals eat it / Sara Levine ; illustrated by Florence Weiser.
Description: Minneapolis : Millbrook Press, [2023] | Includes bibliographical references. | Audience: Ages 5-10 | Audience: Grades 2-3 | Summary: "Eating poop is gross! So why do some animals do it? Get the scoop on the surprisingly good reasons animals such as elephants, butterflies, rabbits, robins, and dogs devour disgusting doo-doo!" —Provided by publisher.
Identifiers: LCCN 2022024113 (print) | LCCN 2022024114 (ebook) | ISBN 9781728457963 (library binding) | ISBN 9781728485621 (ebook)
Subjects: LCSH: Animals—Food—Juvenile literature. | Animal droppings—Juvenile literature. | Animal behavior—Juvenile literature.
Classification: LCC QL756.5 .L48 2023 (print) | LCC QL756.5 (ebook) | DDC 591.5/3—dc23/eng/20220610

LC record available at https://lccn.loc.gov/2022024113
LC ebook record available at https://lccn.loc.gov/2022024114

Manufactured in the United States of America
1-50824-50163-9/8/2022

What's for breakfast?

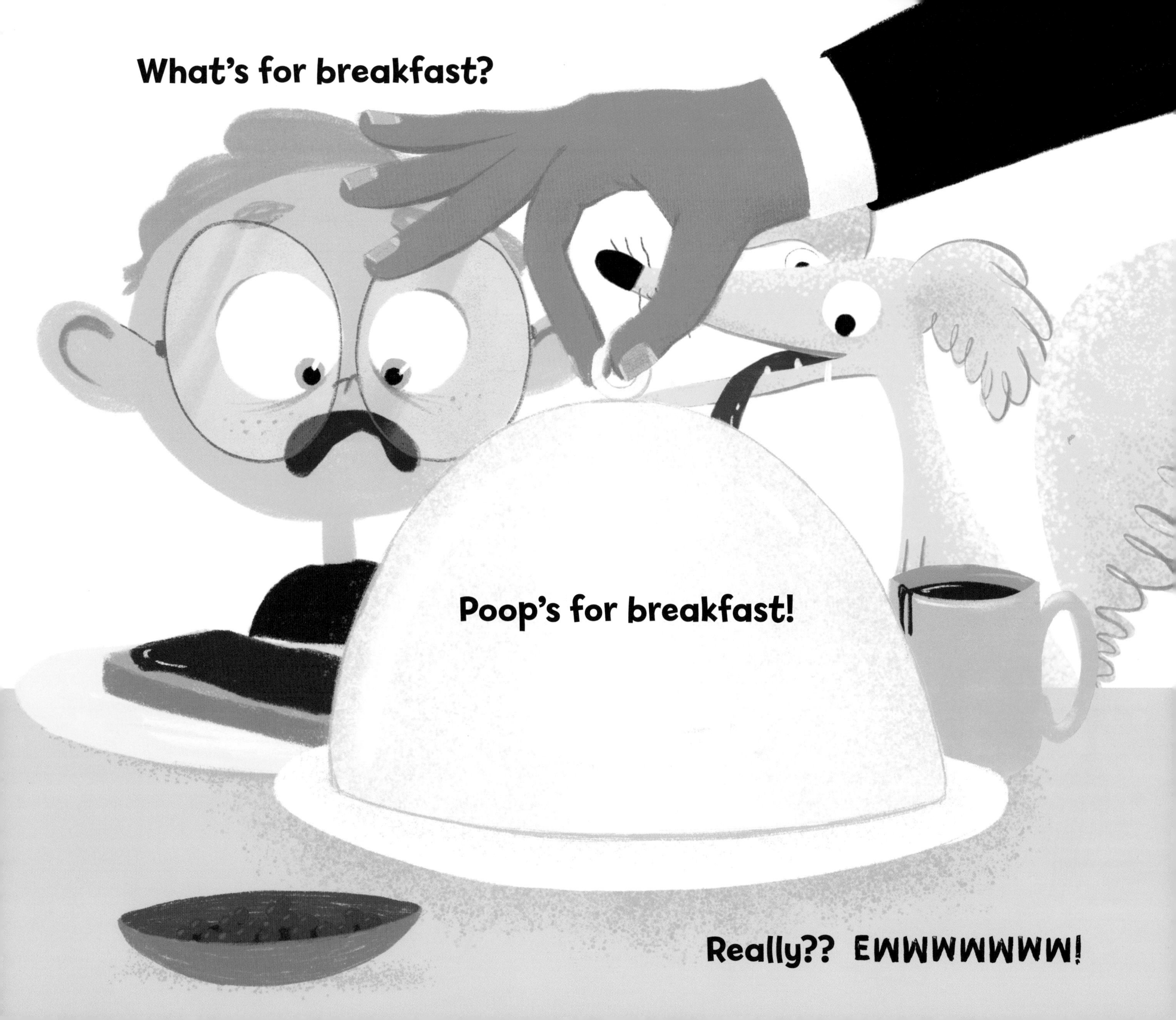

Poop's for breakfast!

Really?? EWWWWWWW!

Well, for some animals, it's no joke.

The practice of eating poop is so common it even has
a name: *coprophagy*.

[kuh-PRAH-fuh-gee]

Why do animals do this?

For a number of surprisingly good reasons.

For some animals, eating poop is part of being a good parent.

Eating poop can help make eggs stronger.

Butterflies usually dine on nectar and fruit. But when a male butterfly comes across a pile of manure, he will probably unwind its proboscis to dig in. Or, more accurately, slurp it up. Male butterflies collect salt in poop to give to female butterflies when they mate. The extra salt increases the chances their babies will hatch and survive.

This behavior in butterflies is called mud puddling. Some other types of insects such as locusts and leafhoppers also do this.

Or it can keep a nest clean and tidy.

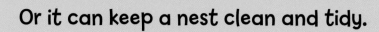

Baby birds eat a lot, so they poop a lot—which could make a nest very dirty. But robins and some other nesting birds have a way around this. Their chicks' poop and pee come out inside a bag made of mucus. It's called a fecal sac. Bird parents grasp it with their beaks and carry it away like a disposable diaper. And sometimes the parents eat it. How come? The poop of a newly hatched chick is full of undigested nutrients.

Eating poop can protect
a baby from predators.

Puppies and kittens are very vulnerable
when they're born. Their eyes are sealed
shut, and they can't hear. They can't even
go to the bathroom on their own. Their
mothers lick them to make them poop
and pee. Then the mothers eat it up, so
the scent doesn't attract animals that
might try to attack or eat the babies.

Some animals eat poop
to help digest food that's
hard to break down.

It takes a lot of work to digest certain types of food like grass, leafy bushes, and tree bark. So elephants get help from bacteria that lives inside their digestive system. To get these bacteria inside their bodies, baby elephants eat poop from their mothers or other herd members. This arrangement works well for the elephants and the bacteria. The elephants get the nutrition they need, and the bacteria gain a safe place to live and food to eat. When two different living things have an arrangement like this that helps both of them out, it's called a symbiotic relationship.

Other baby animals that eat poop to bring bacteria into their bodies to help with digestion include giant pandas, koalas, and hippopotamuses.

Wood is especially difficult to eat.

As their name suggests, wood termites eat wood. And just like elephants, wood termites need some help breaking down their food. Their helpers are tiny, one-celled living things called protozoa. To bring the protozoa inside their bodies, baby termites eat poop from the adults. But there's a difference between the termite and the elephant—for a termite, this behavior doesn't stop as it grows up. Here's why: Whenever an insect grows, it must shed its skin, or molt. Termites, being insects, molt frequently. And each time they do, the protozoa in their digestive tract die and must be replaced. After each molt, these insects need a bit of poop to help them out.

Some animals need food to travel through their bodies two times for them to get all the nutrients out. This can happen because their digestive tracts are very short.

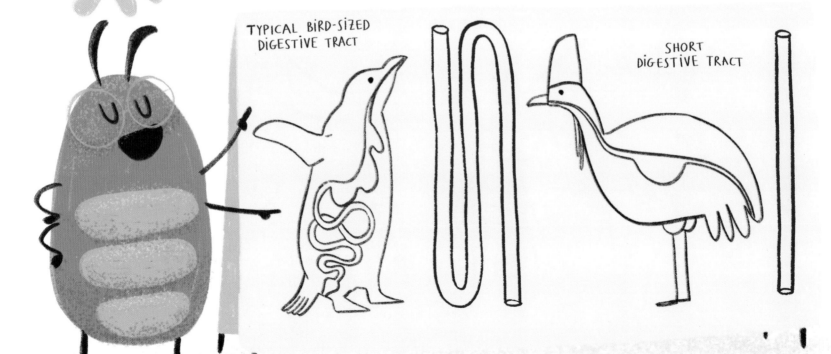

TYPICAL BIRD-SIZED DIGESTIVE TRACT

SHORT DIGESTIVE TRACT

Most animals have a digestive tract that looks like a long tube starting at the mouth and ending at the anus. The tube is all folded up inside the body, but if you removed it and stretched it out, it would be one long tube. A cassowary has a digestive tract that's unusually short for the size of its body. So food has to go through twice for it to break down into small enough pieces to get absorbed. How to accomplish this? The cassowary eats its own poop to send it through a second time. It occasionally pecks through a friend's poop to find undigested morsels as well.

Or it can happen because their digestive tracts are shaped in an unusual way.

Rabbits are hind-gut fermenters. This means a key place where food gets broken down into nutrients is at the end of their digestive tract. This place, the cecum, is located after the small intestine, the place where nutrients go into the body. Since a digestive tract is a one-way street, the nutrients can't back up. Instead, rabbits must poop them out and eat them again.

Do you live with a rabbit? If so, you've probably noticed their poop looks like little round balls. This is the poop that has been though their digestive tracts a second time. The first poop comes out soft, sticky, and full of nutrients. It's called a cecotrope (SEE-ca-trope). Rabbits gobble it up when it comes out at night. That's why you don't see it.

Other hind-gut fermenters that eat their poop include guinea pigs, hamsters, chinchillas, and rats.

ESOPHAGUS

STOMACH

SMALL INTESTINE

CECUM/HIND-GUT

LARGE INTESTINE

ANUS

Some animals eat poop because, well, it's the only option. It's what's for breakfast. And lunch and dinner too!

Dung beetles eat poop because it's the only thing available to eat. And it's also what their home is made of. These insects are born in a house of poop. They eat from the walls until they are ready to emerge into the world. Here's how it works: A parent dung beetle gathers poop, mostly from plant-eating animals such as cows or elephants, and rolls the poop, or dung, into a ball. Then the mother dung beetle lays one fertilized egg in the middle of the ball. When the larva hatches, this offspring has a safe home with plenty of food.

Do adult dung beetles eat dung too? Some do and some don't. There are many different types of this beetle found all over the world, on every continent except Antarctica. They each have different diets and behaviors.

Do some animals eat poop because they just like how it tastes? It's hard to say because they can't tell us.

It does seem like many dogs like to eat poop even when they are not parenting, so maybe this is the case for them. Or perhaps they are trying to get something from poop that is missing from their diets. Scientists are still investigating this question.

There are many good reasons to eat poop.

And so many different types of animals do it.

So is it odd that humans don't?

Nah.

Our digestive tracts work perfectly fine without doing this.

Eating poop will *not* help our babies!

We have diapers to contain the poop. And soap and water or wipes to clean off our babies.

While we do have good bacteria living in our digestive tract to help break down food, we don't need to eat poop to get it there. We bring this helpful bacteria inside our bodies by eating regular food and by picking it up from our surroundings.

Our digestive tract is effective in size and shape. It's long enough that our food gets well digested the first time through. And we are not hind-gut fermenters, so our food gets all broken down before it enters the part of our intestine where the nutrients get absorbed.

Plus, we have *plenty* of tastier options for meals.

Want to guess the number one reason why we don't eat number two?

And we have good reason to think so. Poop contains germs that can make us sick. That's why it's a good idea to wash hands after going to the bathroom or changing a baby's diaper.

So, yes, we find poop gross. But that doesn't mean it's not interesting to learn about. Or an essential part of a healthy diet for other animals. Or even, possibly, delicious!

THE SCOOP ON POOP

What exactly is poop anyway? It's the stuff that comes out of the anus, the end of the digestive tract.

How is it formed? Think of the digestive tract as a tube that's folded up in certain places. It looks different in different types of animals, but it is basically one long tube. Food goes in the mouth, and the body works on it as it goes through the tube. In some places along the tube, stuff comes in to break the food down into smaller bits. In other places along the tube, the small bits get taken out of the tube and enter into the rest of the body. These nutrients give all the cells in the body the energy they need to do their jobs. What's left over at the end of the trip? That's the poop. (Plus, some helpful bacteria along for the ride that got picked up where they live and help out with digestion.)

So then, what is pee? Pee is made up of toxic stuff in the blood plus extra water the body doesn't need. These things are filtered out of the body by kidneys. Pee gets stored in an organ called a bladder, and when it's time to pee, it comes out of a tiny hole called the urethra.

Do most animals poop and pee? Yes.

Do all animals have an anus and a urethra? No, not all of them. Birds have just one opening for poop and pee (and for laying eggs too). This hole is called a cloaca. Reptiles, amphibians, and some mammals, such as the platypus, have a cloaca too.

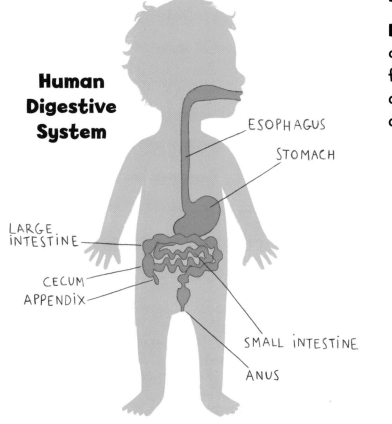

Human Digestive System

ESOPHAGUS

STOMACH

LARGE INTESTINE

CECUM

APPENDIX

SMALL INTESTINE

ANUS

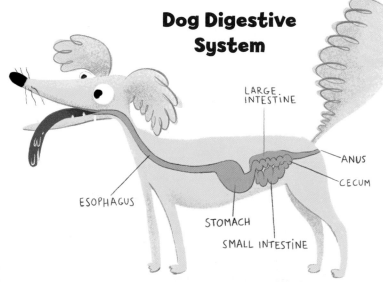

Dog Digestive System

LARGE INTESTINE

ANUS

CECUM

ESOPHAGUS

STOMACH

SMALL INTESTINE

BE A POOP DETECTIVE

Did you know that you can tell if poop is made by a mammal that eats some meat or an animal that eats only plants? It's true! You just need to look at the shape of it. Meat-eater poop comes out larger and is irregularly shaped. Plant-only-eater poop is formed into small round or oval bits.

RABBIT

DEER

DOG

GOAT

HUMAN

CAT

BIRD

In birds, the poop and the pee come out together in one loose dropping. The white part is the pee. The brown part is the poop.

BY ANY OTHER NAME

Here are some synonyms for poop: feces, scat, bowel movement, crap, number two, doo-doo, doody, turd, dung,

FURTHER READING

Gardy, Jennifer. *It Takes Guts: How Your Body Turns Food into Fuel (and Poop)*. Vancouver, BC: Greystone Kids, 2021.

Goodman, Susan E. *The Truth about Poop*. New York: Viking, 2004.

Lunde, Darrin P. *Whose Poop Is That?* Watertown, MA: Charlesbridge, 2017.

Macaulay, David. *Toilet: How It Works*. New York: David Macaulay Studio, 2013.

Paeff, Colleen. *The Great Stink: How Joseph Bazalgette Solved London's Poop Problem*. New York: Margaret K. McElderry Books, 2021.

Parker, Steve. *Digestion*. Chicago: Raintree, 2004.

Stille, Darlene R. *The Digestive System*. New York: Children Press, 1997.

Stokes, Donald W., and Lillian Q. Stokes. *A Guide to Animal Tracking and Behavior*. Boston: Little, Brown, 1986.